The Junior Class
February 14, 1947

Sonnets from the Portuguese

A mystic shape did move behind me.

ELIZABETH BARRETT BROWNING

Sonnets
from the Portuguese

WITH ILLUSTRATIONS BY
WILLY POGANY

New York · THOMAS Y. CROWELL COMPANY · Publishers

Contents

Index to First Lines

List of Color Plates

Introduction

REALITY never before flung itself at once so throbbingly and so exaltingly into any love lyrics as in the "Sonnets." Read all there are in English verse before 1846, and then turn to these by this modern Catarina to her Camoëns, and the alivest of them seem to be artistically contrived reflections of a waned emotional moment. Hers are nobler than the noblest, and yet unflawed by any sense of a creative past tense.

Like a single artless outpour the song rises, yet it has a traceable framework of design; and the "Letters of Robert Browning and Elizabeth Barrett" verify the fact of a foundation for every one of them upon successive actualities in the lovers' relations.

Love and poetic genius together have reconstituted this Realism into an undying Word.

The opening and the closing sonnets are separable from the rest so far as may be. The preluding strain sounds out the main theme, and the dedicatory conclusion places the completed scroll between the lover's hands. The culminating moments are marked in Sonnets 5 and 10, 16, 22, and 27, and in 43. Each triumphs upon a height climbed toward step by step, past the lesser heights of preceding ranges of changing feeling. Through all is movement, growth in riper love.

With the dramatic force of a scene that is the key to all that follows,—especially so in the contrast drawn between belief in Death and the faith in Life which Love calls for,—the action, as it were, of the love-story is unveiled in the first sonnet. It consists in the electrifying apparition of Love in a withdrawn life, so electrifying that its recognition, because of its thrilling import, is sceptically greeted. The mighty images of the goddess-forms of the processional past years, and of a "mystic shape" of supreme mastery in the future, fill the stage with omen or else with promise.

11

Obstacles, only obstacles in love's path, the following three sonnets sing; misapprehension of God's purpose in life for her; disaccord between her stinted possibilities in life, and therefore in art, and those of her lover. Then her adverse view of the fate separating them is delicately interwound in the next three sonnets with more responsive chords of feeling.

The danger of her "Yes" breaks out in Sonnet 5. Its stately metaphor of Electra and her sepulchral urn is splendidly handled to imply the slow solemn glow of hope which the chain of Sonnets 8-12 ring the changes of debate upon, through the successive links of what she can give in return; if she ought in generousness to give it; if love can so exalt the unfit; till, in Sonnet 10, her own answering love asserts itself and rises, love-transfigured, to a corresponding height.

The dependence of her love upon his initiation carries the thought on somewhat hesitatingly through moods that falter and shrink from adequate answer in 11-13; that ask and yield a purely spiritual devotion in 14 and 15, until the goal of a whole-hearted consent is reached in 16.

Too passive a goal is this for the fervor of her awakening devotion. It climbs upward in 17; past the pair of sonnets that celebrate the exchange of the locks of hair; past recapitulating memories of his advent and his declaration, and attains the glory of the love that sings a kindred soul out to his face in the supreme Sonnet 22. So essentially equal and active a love between woman and man was probably never before recorded in a lyric.

In the strength of that climax comes thence the recoil full circle against the original faint-heartedness of the opening sonnets, Sonnet 27 declaring in perfect opposition to their doubt of love and life the equal strength of Love with Death. Death is abjured, postponed, defied as no conqueror now, if it does come, the past is belittled and the future confidently rested upon in the preceding sonnets leading up to this; after which,—with hopeful face set forward, away from what life was before they met,—moment after moment of exultation follows, in alternating wave-like expressions of incidents in their acknowledged love, his letters, her thoughts of him, her mental image of him in his absence, the better reality of his return, the memory of her conquered fears, the sound of her pet name in his voice, and with that sound all that the fusing of her past in this present means; and so on till the crown is set on all with the declaration unfurled with unreserved frankness in Sonnet 43. The dedication of the series to him follows and consummates the whole.

The bare turnings of the construction-walls of the "Sonnets" may be threaded thus; but the golden intimacy of companionship within the house, the flowers and fragrance, the pictures and imagery flexible to every throbbing of living personal impulse,—this is not meant to be dissevered from the impression given.

It is an artistic miracle, fusing within the mind of the reader the spontaneousness of warm-blooded life with the polished fixity of highly conscious poetry.

I never gave a lock of hair away
to a man, Dearest, except this to thee,
Which now upon my fingers thoughtfully
I ring out to the full brown length and say
'Take it.' My day of youth went yesterday —
My hair no longer bounds to my foot's glee,
Nor plant I it from rose or myrtle-tree
As girls do, any more. It only may
Now shade on two pale cheeks, the mark of tear,
Taught drooping from the head that hangs aside
Through sorrow's trick. I thought the funeral-shears
Would take this first, — but love is justified
Take it, thou, ... finding pure from all those years
The kiss my mother left here when she died

Facsimile of Sonnet 18, from Mrs. Browning's manuscript.

One

I thought once how Theocritus had sung
Of the sweet years, the dear and wished-for years,
Who each one in a gracious hand appears
To bear a gift for mortals, old or young:
And, as I mused it in his antique tongue,
I saw, in gradual vision through my tears,
The sweet, sad years, the melancholy years,
Those of my own life, who by turns had flung
A shadow across me. Straightway I was 'ware,
So weeping, how a mystic shape did move
Behind me, and drew me backward by the hair;
And a voice said in mastery, while I strove,—
"Guess now who holds thee?"—"Death," I said. But,
      there,
The silver answer rang,—"Not Death, but Love."

Two

But only three in all God's universe
Have heard this word thou hast said,—Himself,
 beside
Thee speaking, and me listening! and replied
One of us . . . *that* was God, . . . and laid the curse
So darkly on my eyelids, as to amerce
My sight from seeing thee,—that if I had died,
The deathweights, placed there, would have signified
Less absolute exclusion. "Nay" is worse
From God than from all others, O my friend!
Men could not part us with their worldly jars,
Nor the seas change us, nor the tempests bend;
Our hands would touch for all the mountain bars:
And, heaven being rolled between us at the end,
We should but vow the faster for the stars.

Three

Unlike are we, unlike, O princely Heart!
Unlike our uses and our destinies.
Our ministering two angels look surprise
On one another, as they strike athwart
Their wings in passing. Thou, bethink thee, art
A quest for queens to social pageantries,
With gages from a hundred brighter eyes
Than tears even can make mine, to play thy part
Of chief musician. What hast *thou* to do
With looking from the lattice-lights at me,
A poor, tired, wandering singer, singing through
The dark, and leaning up a cypress tree?
The chrism is on thine head,—on mine, the dew,—
And Death must dig the level where these agree.

Four

Thou hast thy calling to some palace-floor,
Most gracious singer of high poems! where
The dancers will break footing, from the care
Of watching up thy pregnant lips for more.
And dost thou lift this house's latch too poor
For hand of thine? and canst thou think and bear
To let thy music drop here unaware
In folds of golden fulness at my door?
Look up and see the casement broken in,
The bats and owlets builders in the roof!
My cricket chirps against thy mandolin.
Hush, call no echo up in further proof
Of desolation! there's a voice within
That weeps . . . as thou must sing . . . alone, aloof.

Five

I lift my heavy heart up solemnly,
As once Electra her sepulchral urn,
And, looking in thine eyes, I overturn
The ashes at thy feet. Behold and see
What a great heap of grief lay hid in me,
And how the red wild sparkles dimly burn
Through the ashen greyness. If thy foot in scorn
Could tread them out to darkness utterly,
It might be well perhaps. But if instead
Thou wait beside me for the wind to blow
The grey dust up, . . . those laurels on thine head
O my Belovèd, will not shield thee so,
That none of all the fires shall scorch and shred
The hair beneath. Stand farther off then! go.

Six

Go from me. Yet I feel that I shall stand
Henceforward in thy shadow. Nevermore
Alone upon the threshold of my door
Of individual life, I shall command
The uses of my soul, nor lift my hand
Serenely in the sunshine as before,
Without the sense of that which I forbore—
Thy touch upon the palm. The widest land
Doom takes to part us, leaves thy heart in mine
With pulses that beat double. What I do
And what I dream include thee, as the wine
Must taste of its own grapes. And when I sue
God for myself, He hears that name of thine,
And sees within my eyes the tears of two.

I shall stand henceforward in thy shadow.

Seven

The face of all the world is changed, I think,
Since first I heard the footsteps of thy soul
Move still, oh, still, beside me, as they stole
Betwixt me and the dreadful outer brink
Of obvious death, where I, who thought to sink,
Was caught up into love, and taught the whole
Of life in a new rhythm. The cup of dole
God gave for baptism, I am fain to drink,
And praise its sweetness, Sweet, with thee anear.
The names of country, heaven, are changed away
For where thou art or shalt be, there or here;
And this . . . this lute and song . . . loved yesterday,
(The singing angels know) are only dear
Because thy name moves right in what they say.

Eight

What can I give thee back, O liberal
And princely giver, who has brought the gold
And purple of thine heart, unstained, untold,
And laid them on the outside of the wall
For such as I to take or leave withal,
In unexpected largesse? am I cold,
Ungrateful, that for these most manifold
High gifts, I render nothing back at all?
Not so; not cold,—but very poor instead.
Ask God who knows. For frequent tears have run
The colours from my life, and left so dead
And pale a stuff, it were not fitly done
To give the same as pillow to thy head.
Go farther! let it serve to trample on.

Nine

Can it be right to give what I can give
To let thee sit beneath the fall of tears
As salt as mine, and hear the sighing years
Re-sighing on my lips renunciative
Through those infrequent smiles which fail to live
For all thy adjurations? O my fears,
That this can scarce be right! We are not peers,
So to be lovers; and I own, and grieve,
That givers of such gifts as mine are, must
Be counted with the ungenerous. Out, alas!
I will not soil thy purple with my dust,
Nor breathe my poison on thy Venice-glass,
Nor give thee any love—which were unjust.
Beloved, I only love thee! let it pass.

Ten

Yet, love, mere love, is beautiful indeed
And worthy of acceptation. Fire is bright,
Let temple burn, or flax; an equal light
Leaps in the flame from cedar-plank or weed:
And love is fire. And when I say at need
I love thee . . . mark! . . . *I love thee*—in thy sight
I stand transfigured, glorified aright,
With conscience of the new rays that proceed
Out of my face toward thine. There's nothing low
In love, when love the lowest: meanest creatures
Who love God, God accepts while loving so.
And what I *feel*, across the inferior features
Of what I *am*, doth flash itself, and show
How that great work of Love enhances Nature's.

Eleven

And therefore if to love can be desert,
I am not all unworthy. Cheeks as pale
As these you see, and trembling knees that fail
To bear the burden of a heavy heart,—
This weary minstrel-life that once was girt
To climb Aornus, and can scarce avail
To pipe now 'gainst the valley nightingale
A melancholy music,—why advert
To these things? O Belovèd, it is plain
I am not of thy worth nor for thy place!
And yet, because I love thee, I obtain
From that same love this vindicating grace,
To live on still in love, and yet in vain,—
To bless thee, yet renounce thee to thy face.

Twelve

Indeed this very love which is my boast,
And which, when rising up from breast to brow,
Doth crown me with a ruby large enow
To draw men's eyes and prove the inner cost,—
This love even, all my worth, to the uttermost,
I should not love withal, unless that thou
Hadst set me an example, shown me how,
When first thine earnest eyes with mine were crossed,
And love called love. And thus, I cannot speak
Of love even, as a good thing of my own:
Thy soul hath snatched up mine all faint and weak,
And placed it by thee on a golden throne,—
And that I love (O soul, we must be meek!)
Is by thee only, whom I love alone.

Thy soul hath snatched up mine.

Thirteen

And wilt thou have me fashion into speech
The love I bear thee, finding words enough,
And hold the torch out, while the winds are rough,
Between our faces, to cast light on each?—
I drop it at thy feet. I cannot teach
My hand to hold my spirit so far off
From myself—me—that I should bring thee proof
In words, of love hid in me out of reach.
Nay, let the silence of my womanhood
Commend my woman-love to thy belief,—
Seeing that I stand unwon, however wooed,
And rend the garment of my life, in brief,
By a most dauntless, voiceless fortitude,
Lest one touch of this heart convey its grief.

Fourteen

If thou must love me, let it be for nought
Except for love's sake only. Do not say
"I love her for her smile—her look—her way
Of speaking gently,—for a trick of thought
That falls in well with mine, and certes brought
A sense of pleasant ease on such a day"—
For these things in themselves, Belovèd, may
Be changed, or change for thee,—and love, so wrought,
May be unwrought so. Neither love me for
Thine own dear pity's wiping my cheeks dry,—
A creature might forget to weep, who bore
Thy comfort long, and lose thy love thereby!
But love me for love's sake, that evermore
Thou mayst love on, through love's eternity.

Fifteen

Accuse me not, beseech thee, that I wear
Too calm and sad a face in front of thine;
For we two look two ways, and cannot shine
With the same sunlight on our brow and hair.
On me thou lookest with no doubting care,
As on a bee shut in a crystalline;
Since sorrow hath shut me safe in love's divine,
And to spread wing and fly in the outer air
Were most impossible failure, if I strove
To fail so. But I look on thee—on thee—
Beholding, besides love, the end of love,
Hearing oblivion beyond memory;
As one who sits and gazes from above,
Over the rivers to the bitter sea.

Sixteen

And yet, because thou overcomest so,
Because thou art more noble and like a king,
Thou canst prevail against my fears and fling
Thy purple round me, till my heart shall grow
Too close against thine heart henceforth to know
How it shook when alone. Why, conquering
May prove as lordly and complete a thing
In lifting upward, as in crushing low!
And as a vanquished soldier yields his sword
To one who lifts him from the bloody earth,
Even so, Belovèd, I at last record,
Here ends my strife. If *thou* invite me forth,
I rise above abasement at the word.
Make thy love larger to enlarge my worth.

Seventeen

*M*y poet, thou canst touch on all the notes
God set between His After and Before,
And strike up and strike off the general roar
Of the rushing worlds a melody that floats
In a serene air purely. Antidotes
Of medicated music, answering for
Mankind's forlornest uses, thou canst pour
From thence into their ears. God's will devotes
Thine to such ends, and mine to wait on thine.
How, Dearest, wilt thou have me for most use?
A hope, to sing by gladly? or a fine
Sad memory, with thy songs to interfuse?
A shade, in which to sing—of palm or pine?
A grave, on which to rest from singing? Choose.

Eighteen

I never gave a lock of hair away
To a man, Dearest, except this to thee,
Which now upon my fingers thoughtfully,
I ring out to the full brown length and say
"Take it." My day of youth went yesterday;
My hair no longer bounds to my foot's glee,
Nor plant I it from rose or myrtle-tree,
As girls do, any more: it only may
Now shade on two pale cheeks the mark of tears,
Taught drooping from the head that hangs aside
Through sorrow's trick. I thought the funeral-shears
Would take this first, but Love is justified,—
Take it thou,—finding pure, from all those years,
The kiss my mother left here when she died.

Nineteen

The soul's Rialto hath its merchandise;
I barter curl for curl upon that mart,
And from my poet's forehead to my heart
Receive this lock which outweighs argosies,
As purply black, as erst to Pindar's eyes
The dim purpureal tresses gloomed athwart
The nine white Muse-brows. For this counterpart, . . .
The bay-crown's shade, Belovèd, I surmise,
Still lingers on thy curl, it is so black!
Thus, with a fillet of smooth-kissing breath,
I tie the shadows safe from gliding back,
And lay the gift where nothing hindereth;
Here on my heart, as on thy brow, to lack
No natural heat till mine grows cold in death.

Twenty

Belovèd, my Belovèd, when I think
That thou wast in the world a year ago,
What time I sat alone here in the snow
And saw no footprint, heard the silence sink
No moment at thy voice, but, link by link,
Went counting all my chains as if that so
They never could fall off at any blow
Struck by thy possible hand,—why, thus I drink
Of life's great cup of wonder! Wonderful,
Never to feel thee thrill the day or night
With personal act or speech,—nor ever cull
Some prescience of thee with the blossoms white
Thou sawest growing! Atheists are as dull,
Who cannot guess God's presence out of sight.

And saw no footprint.

Twenty-one

Say over again, and yet once over again,
That thou dost love me. Though the word repeated
Should seem "a cuckoo-song," as thou dost treat it,
Remember, never to the hill or plain,
Valley and wood, without her cuckoo-strain
Comes the fresh Spring in all her green completed.
Belovèd, I, amid the darkness greeted
By a doubtful spirit-voice, in that doubt's pain
Cry, "Speak once more—thou lovest!" Who can fear
Too many stars, though each in heaven shall roll,
Too many flowers, though each shall crown the year?
Say thou dost love me, love me, love me—toll
The silver iterance!—only minding, Dear,
To love me also in silence with thy soul.

Twenty-two

When our two souls stand up erect and strong,
Face to face, silent, drawing nigh and nigher,
Until the lengthening wings break into fire
At either curvèd point,—what bitter wrong
Can the earth do to us, that we should not long
Be here contented? Think. In mounting higher,
The angels would press on us and aspire
To drop some golden orb of perfect song
Into our deep, dear silence. Let us stay
Rather on earth, Belovèd,—where the unfit
Contrarious moods of men recoil away
And isolate pure spirits, and permit
A place to stand and love in for a day,
With darkness and the death-hour rounding it.

Twenty-three

Is it indeed so? If I lay here dead,
Wouldst thou miss any life in losing mine?
And would the sun for thee more coldly shine
Because of grave-damps falling round my head?
I marvelled, my Belovèd, when I read
Thy thought so in the letter. I am thine—
But . . . *so* much to thee? Can I pour thy wine
While my hands tremble? Then my soul, instead
Of dreams of death, resumes life's lower range.
Then, love me, Love! look on me—breathe on me!
As brighter ladies do not count it strange,
For love, to give up acres and degree,
I yield the grave for thy sake, and exchange
My near sweet view of Heaven, for earth with thee!

Twenty-four

Let the world's sharpness, like a clasping knife,
Shut in upon itself and do no harm
In this close hand of Love, now soft and warm,
And let us hear no sound of human strife
After the click of the shutting. Life to life—
I lean upon thee, Dear, without alarm,
And feel as safe as guarded by a charm
Against the stab of worldlings, who if rife
Are weak to injure. Very whitely still
The lilies of our lives may reassure
Their blossoms from their roots, accessible
Alone to heavenly dews that drop not fewer,
Growing straight, out of man's reach, on the hill.
God only, who made us rich, can make us poor.

Twenty-five

A heavy heart, Belovèd, have I borne
From year to year until I saw thy face,
And sorrow after sorrow took the place
Of all those natural joys as lightly worn
As the stringed pearls, each lifted in its turn
By a beating heart at dance-time. Hopes apace
Were changed to long despairs, till God's own grace
Could scarcely lift above the world forlorn
My heavy heart. Then *thou* didst bid me bring
And let it drop adown thy calmly great
Deep being! Fast it sinketh, as a thing
Which its own nature doth precipitate,
While thine doth close above it, mediating
Betwixt the stars and the unaccomplished fate.

Twenty-six

I lived with visions for my company
Instead of men and women, years ago,
And found them gentle mates, nor thought to know
A sweeter music than they played to me.
But soon their trailing purple was not free
Of this world's dust, their lutes did silent grow,
And I myself grew faint and blind below
Their vanishing eyes. Then THOU didst come—to be,
Belovèd, what they seemed. Their shining fronts,
Their songs, their splendours (better, yet the same,
As river-water hallowed into fonts),
Met in thee, and from out thee overcame
My soul with satisfaction of all wants:
Because God's gifts put man's best dreams to shame.

Twenty-seven

My own Belovèd, who hast lifted me
From this drear flat of earth where I was thrown,
And, in betwixt the languid ringlets, blown
A life-breath, till the forehead hopefully
Shines out again, as all the angels see,
Before thy saving kiss! My own, my own,
Who camest to me when the world was gone,
And I who looked for only God, found *thee!*
I find thee; I am safe, and strong, and glad.
As one who stands in dewless asphodel
Looks backward on the tedious time he had
In the upper life,—so I, with bosom-swell,
Make witness, here, between the good and bad,
That Love, as strong as Death, retrieves as well.

Twenty-eight

My letters! all dead paper, mute and white!
And yet they seem alive and quivering
Against my tremulous hands which loose the string
And let them drop down on my knee to-night.
This said,—he wished to have me in his sight
Once, as a friend: this fixed a day in spring
To come and touch my hand ... a simple thing,
Yet I wept for it!—this, ... the paper's light ...
Said, *Dear, I love thee;* and I sank and quailed
As if God's future thundered on my past.
This said, *I am thine*—and so its ink has paled
With lying at my heart that beat too fast.
And this ... O Love, thy words have ill availed
If, what this said, I dared repeat at last!

My letters! all dead paper, mute and white!

Twenty-nine

I think of thee!—my thoughts do twine and bud
About thee, as wild vines, about a tree,
Put out broad leaves, and soon there's nought to see
Except the straggling green which hides the wood.
Yet, O my palm-tree, be it understood
I will not have my thoughts instead of thee
Who art dearer, better! Rather, instantly
Renew thy presence; as a strong tree should,
Rustle thy boughs and set thy trunk all bare,
And let these bands of greenery which insphere thee
Drop heavily down,—burst, shattered, everywhere!
Because, in this deep joy to see and hear thee
And breathe within thy shadow a new air,
I do not think of thee—I am too near thee.

Thirty

I see thine image through my tears to-night,
And yet to-day I saw thee smiling. How
Refer the cause?—Belovèd, is it thou
Or I, who makes me sad? The acolyte
Amid the chanted joy and thankful rite
May so fall flat, with pale insensate brow,
On the altar-stair. I hear thy voice and vow,
Perplexed, uncertain, since thou art out of sight,
As he, in his swooning ears, the choir's Amen.
Belovèd, dost thou love? or did I see all
The glory as I dreamed, and fainted when
Too vehement light dilated my ideal,
For my soul's eyes? Will that light come again,
As now these tears come—falling hot and real?

Thou comest! All is said without a word.
I sit beneath thy looks, as children do
In the noon-sun, with souls that tremble through
Their happy eyelids from an unaverred
Yet prodigal inward joy. Behold, I erred
In that last doubt! and yet I cannot rue
The sin most, but the occasion—that we two
Should for a moment stand unministered
By a mutual presence. Ah, keep near and close,
Thou dovelike help! and, when my fears would rise,
With thy broad heart serenely interpose:
Brood down with thy divine sufficiencies
These thoughts which tremble when bereft of those,
Like callow birds left desert to the skies.

The first time that the sun rose on thine oath
To love me, I looked forward to the moon
To slacken all those bonds which seemed too soon
And quickly tied to make a lasting troth.
Quick-loving hearts, I thought, may quickly loathe;
And, looking on myself, I seemed not one
For such man's love!—more like an out-of-tune
Worn viol, a good singer would be wroth
To spoil his song with, and which, snatched in haste,
Is laid down at the first ill-sounding note.
I did not wrong myself so, but I placed
A wrong on *thee*. For perfect strains may float
'Neath master-hands, from instruments defaced,—
And great souls, at one stroke, may do and doat.

For perfect strains may float 'neath master-hands.

Thirty-three

Yes, call me by my pet-name! let me hear
The name I used to run at, when a child,
From innocent play, and leave the cowslips piled,
To glance up in some face that proved me dear
With the look of its eyes. I miss the clear
Fond voices which, being drawn and reconciled
Into the music of Heaven's undefiled,
Call me no longer. Silence on the bier,
While I call God—call God!—So let thy mouth
Be heir to those who are now exanimate.
Gather the north flowers to complete the south,
And catch the early love up in the late.
Yes, call me by that name,—and I, in truth,
With the same heart, will answer and not wait.

Thirty-four

With the same heart, I said, I'll answer thee
As those, when thou shalt call me by my name—
Lo, the vain promise! is the same, the same,
Perplexed and ruffled by life's strategy?
When called before, I told how hastily
I dropped my flowers or brake off from a game,
To run and answer with the smile that came
At play last moment, and went on with me
Through my obedience. When I answer now,
I drop a grave thought, break from solitude;
Yet still my heart goes to thee—ponder how—
Not as to a single good, but all my good!
Lay thy hand on it, best one, and allow
That no child's foot could run fast as this blood.

If I leave all for thee, wilt thou exchange
And be all to me? Shall I never miss
Home-talk and blessing and the common kiss
That comes to each in turn, nor count it strange,
When I look up, to drop on a new range
Of walls and floors, another home than this?
Nay, wilt thou fill that place by me which is
Filled by dead eyes too tender to know change?
That's hardest. If to conquer love, has tried,
To conquer grief, tries more, as all things prove;
For grief indeed is love and grief beside.
Alas, I have grieved so I am hard to love.
Yet love me—wilt thou? Open thine heart wide,
And fold within the wet wings of thy dove.

When we met first and loved, I did not build
Upon the event with marble. Could it mean
To last, a love set pendulous between
Sorrow and sorrow? Nay, I rather thrilled,
Distrusting every light that seemed to gild
The onward path, and feared to overlean
A finger even. And, though I have grown serene
And strong since then, I think that God has willed
A still renewable fear . . . O love, O troth . . .
Lest these enclaspèd hands should never hold,
This mutual kiss drop down between us both
As an unowned thing, once the lips being cold.
And Love, be false! if *he*, to keep one oath,
Must lose one joy, by his life's star foretold.

Thirty-seven

Pardon, oh, pardon, that my soul should make,
Of all that strong divineness which I know
For thine and thee, an image only so
Formed of the sand, and fit to shift and break.
It is that distant years which did not take
Thy sovranty, recoiling with a blow,
Have forced my swimming brain to undergo
Their doubt and dread, and blindly to forsake
Thy purity of likeness and distort
Thy worthiest love to a worthless counterfeit:
As if a shipwrecked Pagan, safe in port,
His guardian sea-god to commemorate,
Should set a sculptured porpoise, gills a-snort
And vibrant tail, within the temple-gate.

Thirty-eight

First time he kissed me, he but only kissed
The fingers of this hand wherewith I write;
And ever since, it grew more clean and white,
Slow to world-greetings, quick with its "Oh, list,"
When the angels speak. A ring of amethyst
I could not wear here, plainer to my sight,
Than that first kiss. The second passed in height
The first, and sought the forehead, and half missed,
Half falling on the hair. O beyond meed!
That was the chrism of love, which love's own crown,
With sanctifying sweetness, did precede.
The third upon my lips was folded down
In perfect, purple state; since when, indeed,
I have been proud and said, "My love, my own."

He but only kissed the fingers of this hand.

Because thou hast the power and own'st the grace
To look through and behind this mask of me
(Against which years have beat thus blanchingly
With their rains), and behold my soul's true face,
The dim and weary witness of life's race,—
Because thou hast the faith and love to see,
Through that same soul's distracting lethargy,
The patient angel waiting for a place
In the new Heavens,—because nor sin nor woe,
Nor God's infliction, nor death's neighbourhood,
Nor all which others viewing, turn to go,
Nor all which makes me tired of all, self-viewed,—
Nothing repels thee, . . . Dearest, teach me so
To pour out gratitude, as thou dost, good!

Forty

Oh, yes! they love through all this world of ours
I will not gainsay love, called love forsooth.
I have heard love talked in my early youth,
And since, not so long back but that the flowers
Then gathered, smell still. Mussulmans and Giaours
Throw kerchiefs at a smile, and have no ruth
For any weeping. Polypheme's white tooth
Slips on the nut if, after frequent showers,
The shell is over-smooth,—and not so much
Will turn the thing called love, aside to hate
Or else to oblivion. But thou art not such
A lover, my Belovèd! thou canst wait
Through sorrow and sickness, to bring souls to touch,
And think it soon when others cry "Too late."

Forty-one

I thank all who have loved me in their hearts,
With thanks and love from mine. Deep thanks to all
Who paused a little near the prison-wall
To hear my music in its louder parts
Ere they went onward, each one to the mart's
Or temple's occupation, beyond call.
But thou, who, in my voice's sink and fall
When the sob took it, thy divinest Art's
Own instrument didst drop down at thy foot
To hearken what I said between my tears, . . .
Instruct me how to thank thee! Oh, to shoot
My soul's full meaning into future years,
That *they* should lend it utterance, and salute
Love that endures, from Life that disappears!

Forty-two

"My future will not copy fair my past"—
I wrote that once; and thinking at my side
My ministering life-angel justified
The word by his appealing look upcast
To the white throne of God, I turned at last,
And there, instead, saw thee, not unallied
To angels in thy soul! Then I, long tried
By natural ills, received the comfort fast,
While budding, at thy sight, my pilgrim's staff
Gave out green leaves with morning dews impearled.
I seek no copy now of life's first half:
Leave here the pages with long musing curled,
And write me new my future's epigraph
New angel mine, unhoped for in the world!

Forty-three

How do I love thee? Let me count the ways.
I love thee to the depth and breadth and height
My soul can reach, when feeling out of sight
For the ends of Being and ideal Grace.
I love thee to the level of everyday's
Most quiet need, by sun and candle-light.
I love thee freely, as men strive for Right;
I love thee purely, as they turn from Praise.
I love thee with the passion put to use
In my old griefs, and with my childhood's faith.
I love thee with a love I seemed to lose
With my lost saints. I love thee with the breath,
Smiles, tears, of all my life!—and, if God choose,
I shall but love thee better after death.

Forty-four

Belovèd, thou hast brought me many flowers
Plucked in the garden, all the summer through
And winter, and it seemed as if they grew
In this close room, nor missed the sun and showers.
So, in the like name of that love of ours,
Take back these thoughts which here unfolded too,
And which on warm and cold days I withdrew
From my heart's ground. Indeed, those beds and bowers
Be overgrown with bitter weeds and rue,
And wait thy weeding; yet here's eglantine,
Here's ivy!—take them, as I used to do
Thy flowers, and keep them where they shall not pine.
Instruct thine eyes to keep their colours true,
And tell thy soul their roots are left in mine.

Yet here's eglantine, here's ivy!

Notes

After Elizabeth Barrett Barrett's marriage to Robert Browning, and when they were fully established at their home in Pisa, these sonnets were first made known, in MS., to Mr. Browning, on this wise, according to Mr. Edmund Gosse, who heard it from Browning himself:

"Their custom was, Mr. Browning said, to write alone, and not to show each other what they had written. This was a rule which he sometimes broke through, but she never. He had the habit of working in a downstairs room, where their meals were spread, while Mrs. Browning studied in a room on the floor above. One day, early in 1847, their breakfast being over, Mrs. Browning went upstairs, while her husband stood at the window watching the street till the table should be cleared. He was presently aware of some one behind him, although the servant was gone. It was Mrs. Browning, who held him by the shoulder to prevent his turning to look at her, and at the same time pushed a packet of papers into the pocket of his coat. She told him to read that, and to tear it up if he did not like it; and then she fled again to her own room. Mr. Browning seated himself at the table and unfolded the parcel. It contained the series of sonnets which have now become so illustrious. As he read, his emotion and delight may be conceived. Before he had finished it was impossible for him to restrain himself, . . . he rushed upstairs, and stormed that guarded citadel. He was early conscious that these were treasures not to be kept from the world. 'I dared not reserve to myself,' he said, 'the finest sonnets written in any language since Shakespeare's.' But Mrs. Browning was very loth indeed to consent to the publication of what had been the very notes and chronicle of her betrothal. At length she was persuaded to permit her friend, Miss Mary Russell Mitford, to whom they had originally been sent in manuscript, to pass them through the press."—"Critical Kit-Kats," p. 2.

Accordingly a thin octavo volume of forty-seven pages was printed, entitled:

Sonnets | by | E. B. B. | Reading. | *Not for Publication* | 1847.

The Sonnets were first published in the edition of 1850, at the close of the second volume, and the title "Sonnets from the Portuguese" was suggested by Robert Browning, and agreed upon as preferable to his wife's suggestion of "Sonnets translated from the Bosnian," with the idea of veiling the authorship and yet acknowledging their connection with the author of "Catarina to Camoëns," whom Robert Browning, who much admired this lyric of hers, used to call his "own little Portuguese" before he knew of the Sonnets.

~ ONE ~

LINE 1. *How Theocritus had sung:* in his Idyl xv., at the beginning of the Adonis song occurring in it. The passage is translated by Mr. Andrew Lang thus: "O Aphrodite, that playest with gold, lo, from the stream eternal of Acheron they have brought back to thee Adonis—even in the twelfth month they have brought him, the dainty-footed Hours. Tardiest of the Immortals are the beloved Hours, but dear and desired they come, for always, to all mortals, they bring some gift with them." The poet was probably not unmindful of the appropriateness of the reference to the Adonis song for still another reason—that it celebrated the return of Spring and the reanimation of Love, and as readers of the Browning Love Letters will notice, their first meeting was in May, and the famous letter from Robert, shortly after, which was destroyed for its plain speaking, evidently was sent May 23, 1845.

5. *In his antique tongue:* Theocritus (born B.C. 315) was born in Syracuse, Sicily, the greatest of the cities of Magna Græcia, and wrote, of course, in Greek.

11. *Drew me backward by the hair:* so Athene, in "Mystic Shape," unseen by those who were with him, drew Achilles "backward by the hair." (See "Iliad," i., 204.)

14. *Not Death, but Love:* the awakening from the invalid's anticipation of death to a growing consciousness of love and all it

77

means is the key theme throughout the sonnets. Compare recurrences of this, 7, *2-6;* 23, *9-10, 13-14;* 27, *8, 14;* 39, *10;* 40, *12-14;* 42, *5, 6;* also Robert Browning's "O Lyric Love" in the "The Ring and the Book," i., 1389, 1390; and "Letters of Robert Browning and Elizabeth Barrett,": "I had done *living*, I thought, when you came and sought me out."

∼ Two ∼

1. *But only three, etc.:* again, perhaps, a veiled allusion to the destroyed letter in which, according to our poet, Robert spoke "wildly," saying "intemperate things . . . fancies" which she begged him to forget at once and let die out between them alone, and so spare her the sadness of having to break through an intercourse promising friendliness and sympathy. (See "The Letters of Robert Browning and Elizabeth Barrett," pp. 74-75, also pp. 221-222, 205, 213.)

5. *To amerce my sight, etc.:* to deprive my sight, a similar use of "amerce" to that in Milton's "Paradise Lost," i., 609: "for his fault, amerced of heaven."

7. *The deathweights:* alluding to the old custom of placing pennies on the eyelids of the dead to keep them closed.

8. *"Nay" is worse from God:* "But that God is stronger than we, cannot be a bitter thought to you but a holy thought," says "E. B. B." in a letter to "R. B.," Sept. 13, 1845, and again, three days later, "Something worse than even a sense of unworthiness, *God* has put between us." (See also "Letters of R. B. and E. B.")

∼ Three ∼

3. *Our ministering two angels:* compare 42, *3, 16.*

8. *To play thy part:* in the edition of 1850 this read "*ply* thy part."

12. *Leaning up:* a form of speech recurring in "watching up," 4, *4.—A cypress tree:* the cypress being associated with death.

13. *The chrism is on thine head,—on mine, the dew:* referring in *the chrism* to the oil of anointing used in coronation, in *the dew*, to the death-damps.

78

~ Four ~

On this and the foregoing sonnet, also sonnets 7, 8, and 9, compare the "Letters of Robert Browning and Elizabeth Barrett," pp. 202, 210, 214, 223, and on.

11. *My cricket chirps against thy mandolin:* "When you were only a poet to me (only a poet: does it sound irreverent? almost, I think!) I used to study characteristic by characteristic, and turn myself round in despair of being ever able to approach," Elizabeth wrote to Robert; and he, at another time, wrote to her of "the strange exalting way you will persist to think of me."

~ Five ~

2. *As once Electra her sepulchral urn:* when Electra receives her brother's funeral urn from the disguised Orestes, who afterward did wait beside her (see line *10* of the sonnet) also, and made known to her how in those ashes there was really life, and only a pretence of death. (See the "Electra" of Sophocles, Plumptre's translation, lines 1126-1229.)

~ Six ~

2. *Nevermore alone, etc.:* this "proof of this regard—all this that you are to me in fact . . . my wonder is greater than your wonder . . . I who sate here alone but yesterday, so weary of my own being." (See "Letters of R. B. and E. B.")

~ Seven ~

7. *The cup of dole:* compare the sonnet "Past and Future."

~ Eight ~

2. *Gold And purple:* meaning riches and beauty—gold being the most precious metal, purple the color of royalty and state. Compare 9, *10;* 16, *4;* 38, *13.*

3. *Untold:* meaning untallied, or uncounted, not unexpressed.

4. *Laid them on the outside of the wall:* how true this is to

the facts between the two poets, the "Love Letters" show.

6. *Largesse:* a public bounty distributed to a crowd. Here, a liberal gift offered as if left outside the door.

— Nine —

1. *Can it be right to give What I can give:* "What can I give you which it would not be ungenerous to give? What should I put into your life," she asks, in one of her letters, "but anxiety and sadness?"

7. *Peers:* used in the original sense of the word, as equals.

12. *Thy Venice-glass:* poison poured in Venetian glass was popularly supposed to shatter it, the quality of such glass being so fine as to feel at once the subtle element of death in the liquid.

— Ten —

8. *With conscience, etc.:* "conscience" is here used in the sense of *consciousness*, the original meaning, now rarely used.

— Eleven —

5. *That once was girt To Climb Aornus:* evidently the "Aornus" meant is not the entrance to Hades fabled to be known by its birdlessness, because of the noxious gases rising, so that birds avoided flying near,—*aornus* meaning birdless,—but the Aornus of India is meant, a lonely, lofty rock whither only the birds of strong pinion soared to.

— Twelve —

3. *Enow:* enough, an obsolete form of the word; compare Omar Khayyám in the Fitzgerald version:

> "A book of verses underneath the bough,
> A loaf of bread, a jug of wine, and Thou
> Singing beside me in the wilderness—
> Oh! wilderness were paradise enow."

— Fourteen —

1. *Let it be for nought Except for love's sake only:* "The first moment in which I seemed to admit to myself . . . the *possibility* of

80

your affection . . . was *that* when you intimated . . . that you cared for me, not for a reason, but because you cared for me. Now such a 'parceque' which reasonable people would take to be irrational was just the only one fitted to the uses of my understanding . . . for if so, it was altogether unanswerable," etc. (See "Love Letters.")

11. *A creature might forget to weep:* in the edition of 1850 this line ran: "Since one might well forget to weep."

~ Fifteen ~

6. *A bee shut in a crystalline:* Dr. W. J. Rolfe, commenting on this line, considers that in using "crystalline" here, as a noun, the poet does not mean a bee shut in a crystal, as a fly in amber, but with a glass vessel over it. But the metaphor is not followed far beyond the mere significance of herself being shut away from the world, and from active life in her invalid room, while the beloved one is free of the sunshine, so that there is no need of restricting the meaning to a glass tumbler over a captured bee; in fact, that is less appropriate, since she has no idea of her imprisonment being temporary as that would be, and elsewhere she uses "crystalline" as a noun, in the sense of a crystal.

7. *Since sorrow, etc.:* in edition of 1850 this read "for sorrow."

~ Sixteen ~

9-10. *And as a vanquished soldier, etc.:* these lines in the edition of 1850 ran,

"And as a soldier struck down by a sword
    May cry, 'My strife ends here,' and sinks to earth,
    Even so," etc.

12. *Strife:* in the first edition was "doubt"! That the new readings are in all ways better than the original is obvious.

~ Seventeen ~

10. *How, Dearest, wilt thou have me for most use?* "Are you not my dear friend already and shall I not use you?" asked Robert Browning in one of his earliest letters before the two had met. ("Letters.")

81

13. *Of palm or pine:* the former associated with life in this relation, the latter with death.

~ Eighteen ~

1. *I never gave a lock of hair . . . except this to thee:* Robert Browning asked for so much of her as might be given in a lock of hair. To this letter of Nov. 24, 1845, she replied the same day that she had never given away what he asked except to nearest relatives, and playfully putting him off while yielding, she wrote again on the 27th: "I *never can* nor *will give you this thing;*—only . . . I will, if you please, exchange it for another thing—you understand . . . I will not pretend to be generous, no, nor 'kind.' It shall be pure merchandise." Thereupon "R. B." the next day answers: "Take it, dearest; what I am forced to think you mean" (see "Letters of R. B. and E. B."), and out of all this, Sonnets 18 and 19 grew.

7. *Nor plant I it from rose or myrtle-tree:* nor does she plant in her hair now sprigs from the rose or the myrtle tree.

10. *The head that hangs aside Through sorrow's trick:* lines that paint herself in accord with her portraits.

11. *I thought the funeral-shears Would take this first:* an allusion to the Greek and Roman custom of cutting the hair at death.

14. *The kiss my mother left here when she died:* Oct. 1, 1828, Mrs. Barrett died.

~ Nineteen ~

1. *The soul's Rialto, etc.:* the Rialto which animates this imagery is doubtless Shakespeare's, and it is the argosies of Antonio which are brought to mind as outweighed by this lock of hair (see "The Merchant of Venice," i., 1, 9, 3, 108). The merchandising of which she speaks is echoed in the love letters making the proposition to barter locks of hair, see foregoing quotation.

5. *As purply black, as erst to Pindar's eyes, etc.:* refers to Pindar's first Pythian ode beginning, "O golden lyre, thou common treasure of Apollo and the Muses violet-tressed," as Myer translates it. This word in the Greek, however, is *ioplakamon,* and

as black is the nearest translation of our *io*, our poet's *purply-black* is a happy gloss upon the original.

~ TWENTY ~

12. *Some prescience of thee with the blossoms white Thou sawest:* a reference to the spring-time when they first met, after many letters had passed between them, more than one of Robert Browning's looking forward to the spring, when Miss Barrett hoped to be enough better to see him, and therefore taking account of winds and signs of spring. "Surely the wind that sets my chestnut-tree dancing, all its baby-cone-blossoms, green now, rocking like fairy castles on a hill in an earthquake,—that is southwest surely!" he writes in a letter of May 3, 1845, which may have been in our poet's mind here.

~ TWENTY-ONE ~

3. *A cuckoo-song:* a common phrase for an unwearying repetition like the cry of that bird.

4. *Never . . . without her cuckoo-strain Comes the fresh Spring:* that the cuckoo's note is the herald of spring in England many an English poet witnesses, notably the nameless writer of the charming old English song, "Sommer is y comin' in, Sing Cuckoo!"

~ TWENTY-TWO ~

3. *The lengthening wings break into fire:* an image suggested by the glory of God present in the mercy-seat of the Ark in the Jewish tabernacle, the mercy-seat being between the wings of the golden angels sculptured above the Ark. (See Exodus xxv., 17-20.)

14. *The death-hour rounding it:* a use of the verb "to round" in the sense of enclosing and completing, like Shakespeare's "Our little life is rounded with a sleep." (See "The Tempest," iv., 1, 158.)

~ TWENTY-FOUR ~

8. *Rife:* meaning ready, an obsolete use of the word, signifying "abundant" in Anglo-Saxon.

~ Twenty-six ~

1. *I lived with visions for my company, etc.:* "I grew up in the country—had no social opportunities, had my heart in books and poetry, and my experience in reveries. . . . Books and dreams were what I lived in. . . . Afterwards, when my illness came . . . then I turned with some bitterness . . . [on my past, realizing] that I had seen no Human Nature."

~ Twenty-seven ~

10. *Dewless·asphodel:* in the fields of Elysium where the flower of immortality, the asphodel, grows. "The meadows thick with asphodel," says Homer. (See "Odyssey," Book xi., 669.)

~ Twenty-eight ~

1. *My letters:* which are now the world's and no less hers. (See the "Letters of Robert Browning and Elizabeth Barrett," Vols. i. and ii., 1899.)

5. *This said, etc.:* the first letter, Jan. 10, 1845.

6. *This fixed a day in spring:* "I will call at two on Tuesday," "R. B." wrote in a letter of May 17, 1845.

8. *Yet I wept for it:* "When I wrote that letter to let you come the first time, do you know, the tears ran down my cheeks.—I could not tell why: partly it might be mere nervousness. And then I was vexed with you for wishing to come as other people did, and vexed with myself for not being able to refuse you as I did them." —*This . . . said,* Dear, I love thee: if one may trace the rich windings of this labyrinth of love, reverently, it is the letter of August 30 that is thus referred to.

11. *This said,* I am thine: in such letters, our poets were rich, yet the first is perhaps meant, the letter of September 13.

~ Thirty ~

2. *How Refer the cause:* "refer" here is used in the sense of tracing back an effect to its cause—how account for its origin.

~ Thirty-one ~

4. *Unaverred:* meaning unconfessed, left unasserted or affirmed, the word "aver" being derived from the Latin *ad,* to, and *verum,* truth.

~ Thirty-two ~

3. *Bonds which seemed too . . . quickly tied to make a lasting troth:* compare Sonnet 36.

12. *Perfect strains . . . from instruments defaced:* compare the thought of Robert Browning's "My Star": "What matter to me if their Star is a world," etc.

~ Thirty-three ~

1. *Yes, call me by my pet-name:* see "The Pet Name." "But I *have* a new thing to say or sing—you never before heard me love and bless and send my heart after—'Ba'—did you? Ba—and that is you! I TRIED—(more than *wanted*) to call you that on Wednesday." So wrote Robert, and Elizabeth replied, "I am *glad* you do not despise my own right name too much, because I never was called Elizabeth by any one who loved me at all, and I accept the omen." Again in 1847 she wrote of Robert's always calling her *Ba* and thinking it the prettiest name in the world, which might be considered a proof not only of blind love but of deaf love.

6. *Voices which . . . Call me no longer:* her mother's, and her favorite brother's, Edward, who was drowned July, 1841, in Babbicombe Bay.

10. *Exanimate:* no longer animate, lifeless, used in the original sense, as in "Spenser's Faerie Queene," ii., 12, 7, "carkass exanimate."

~ Thirty-seven ~

10. *Thy worthiest love to:* in the edition of 1850 reads "Thy worthiest love with."

11. *A shipwrecked Pagan, safe in port, etc.:* refers to the custom of giving to the god through whom came deliverance a statue in the temple, as a votive offering. Such a piece must be but a travesty of the power and majesty of the god himself.

85

~ FORTY ~

5. *Giaours:* infidels, Saracens or Turks, Orientals, that is, whose love is that of the mere possession of beauty, who are allured by gayety, cruel despite tears.

7. *Polypheme's white tooth:* Polyphemus, the Cyclops, one-eyed giant son of Neptune, who was in love with Galatea, the sea-nymph, in a crude and petulant way; but she, scoffing at his one eye and shaggy eyebrow, escaped him, hence the image of the white tooth of his appetite slipping on the coveted kernel.

~ FORTY-ONE ~

14. *Love that endures, from Life that disappears:* the "from" was "with" in edition of 1850.

~ FORTY-TWO ~

1. *My future will not copy fair my past:* quoted from the sonnet entitled "Past and Future." Concerning it Robert Browning wrote her, November, 1845, that it affected him more than any poem he ever read. "May God bless me, as you pray, by letting that beloved hand shake the less—I will only ask, *the less*—for being laid on mine through this life," and she answered with this sonnet, and in the Letters also, calling him her "angel," thus: "nor say, that I 'do not lean' on you with all the weight of my 'past'—because I do!" This sonnet did not appear in the edition of 1850, but was inserted between 41 and the following sonnet, in the reissue of the "Works" in 3 vols., 1856.

~ FORTY-FOUR ~

This and the preceding sonnet were numbered respectively 43 and 42 in the edition of 1850. The flowers of which this closing sonnet speaks are referred to continuously throughout the "Love Letters." She writes in one case that her brothers say, "Ah, you had Mr. Browning with you yesterday. I see by the flowers, just as if they said, I see Queen Mab has been with you."

9. *Be overgrown:* the "Be" is here used in the sense of *are* and in the Elizabethan manner, as in "Hamlet," iii., 2, 32, "O there be players that I have seen," etc.